A player tackles another player.

Jim Brown

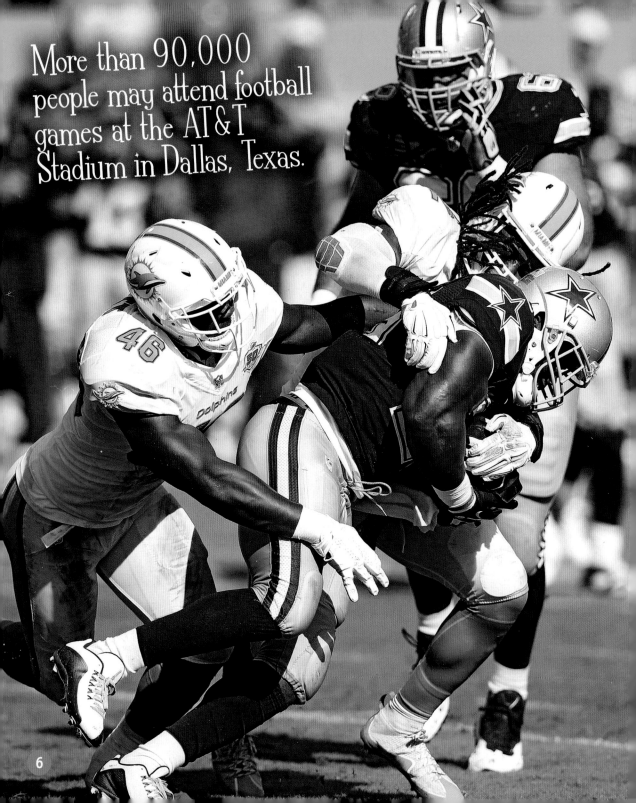

More than 90,000 people may attend football games at the AT&T Stadium in Dallas, Texas.

Being Your Best at Football

NEL YOMTOV

Children's Press®
An Imprint of Scholastic Inc.

Content Consultant
Barry Wilner
Associated Press
New York City, New York

Library of Congress Cataloging-in-Publication Data
Names: Yomtov, Nelson.
Title: Being your best at football / by Nel Yomtov.
Description: New York : Children's Press An Imprint of Scholastic Inc., 2016.
| ? 2017. | Series: A True Book | Includes bibliographical references and index.
Identifiers: LCCN 2015048508| ISBN 9780531232644 (library binding) |
ISBN 9780531236154 (paperback)
Subjects: LCSH: Football—United States—Juvenile literature. |
  Football—United States—History—Juvenile literature.
Classification: LCC GV950.7 .Y67 2016 | DDC 796.332—dc23
LC record available at http://lccn.loc.gov/2015048508

© 2017 Scholastic Inc.
All rights reserved. Published in 2017 by Children's Press, an imprint of Scholastic Inc.
Printed in China 62
SCHOLASTIC, CHILDREN'S PRESS, A TRUE BOOK™, and associated logos are trademarks and/or registered trademarks of Scholastic Inc.
1 2 3 4 5 6 7 8 9 10 R 26 25 24 23 22 21 20 19 18 17

Front cover: A player jumping to catch a football
Back cover: A team celebrating

Find the Truth!

Everything you are about to read is true *except* for one of the sentences on this page.

Which one is **TRUE?**

T or F Players are required to wear protective gear when playing football.

T or F Only men play professional football.

Find the answers in this book.

Contents

THE **BIG** TRUTH!

A player with the Independent
Women's Football League
preparing to pass the ball

4

A Game Called Football

Football is one of the most popular and exciting games in the United States. Each week during football season, hundreds of thousands of fans visit stadiums to watch high school, college, and **professional** teams play. Millions more follow the action on television. This American-born game features strategy, bone-jarring hits, blazing speed, and fancy footwork. Football can also be a fun game to play. And with dedication and practice, you can become the best player you can be!

Prepare for Battle

Football is a rough-and-tumble **contact sport**. It requires players to wear protective equipment and gear. A helmet made of unbreakable plastic with a face mask and chinstrap is a must. A well-fitting mouth guard helps protect a player's teeth. Pads protect the shoulders, hips, and ribs. Thigh pads and knee pads are worn inside specially made football pants. Players also wear football **cleats** to grip the grassy field better. The shoes help them avoid slipping when making quick, sharp changes in direction.

Helmet

Mouth guard

Pads

Pants with padding

Cleats

Good padding provides some protection to a football player.

Speed and agility are useful skills for anyone on the field.

The Right Stuff

Football players come in all body types and sizes. Some positions benefit from size and strength. Others better suit players built for speed or who have "soft" hands to catch a ball without letting it bounce out of their grip. For any player, quickness and **endurance** are important. Alertness, cleverness, and the ability to fake out your **opponent** are also great skills.

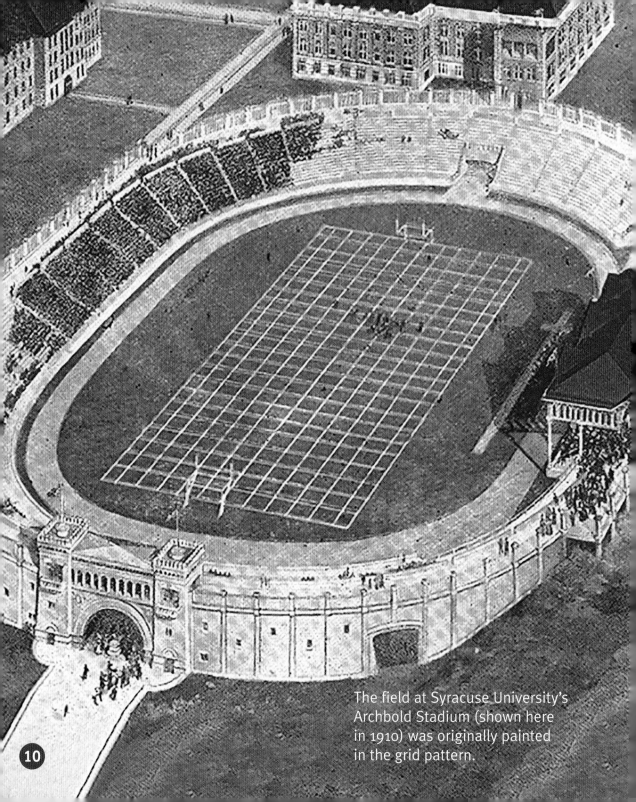

The field at Syracuse University's Archbold Stadium (shown here in 1910) was originally painted in the grid pattern.

Hit the Gridiron!

A football field is often called a **gridiron**. The term comes from early football fields, which were marked in a checkerboard, or grid, pattern. The name stuck even after the grid pattern was no longer used. Most professional football fields are outdoors and have grass surfaces. Indoor fields have **synthetic** turf surfaces. Modern turf uses soft fibers and tiny pieces of shredded car tires to soften the impact on players' bodies.

Football first developed among American universities.

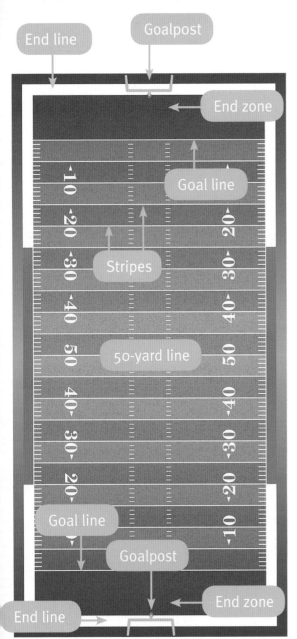

Numbers on a football field label every 10 yards. Team or city names usually fill the end zones.

The Playing Field

A football field is 120 yards (110 meters) long and 53$\frac{1}{3}$ yards (49 m) wide. Parallel lines called stripes, set 5 yards (4.6 m) apart, divide the field. The final line at each of the two ends of the field is called the end line. Ten yards (9 m) before each end line is the goal line. The two goal lines are 100 yards (91.4 m) apart. The area between the end line and the goal line is the end zone.

Each end zone has a goalpost shaped like a huge letter *H*. The horizontal bar is called the crossbar. The vertical poles are called uprights.

The 50-yard line runs across the middle of the field and divides it into two equal territories. Each team guards its own territory. To score, a team moves the ball into the opponent's end zone (a touchdown) or kicks it through the goalpost (a field goal).

Hash marks are short stripes placed 1 yard (0.9 m) apart on the playing field.

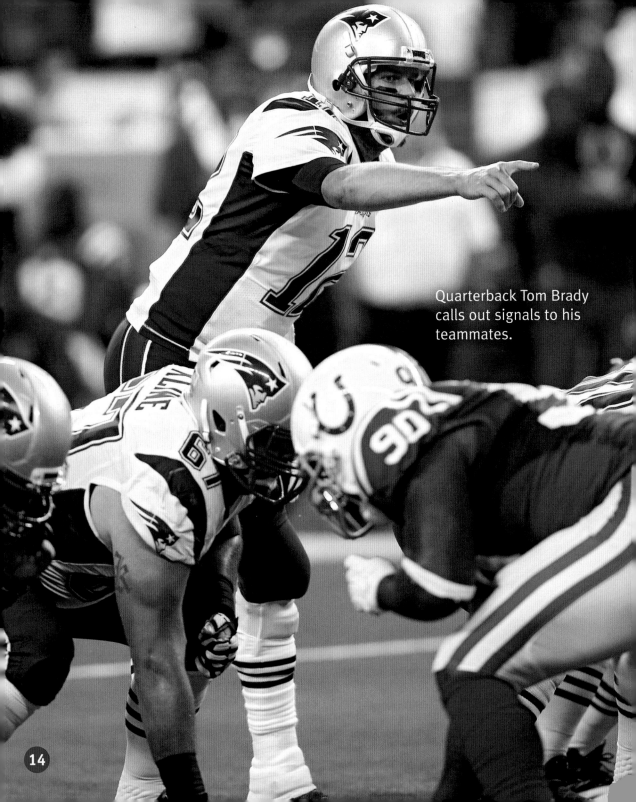

Quarterback Tom Brady calls out signals to his teammates.

CHAPTER 3

The Players

Each team has 11 players on the field at one time. The team moving the ball toward its opponent's goal line is called the offense. The team trying to stop the offense from scoring is called the defense. Each player on the offense and the defense has a different job.

Teams in the National Football League (NFL) can have 46 players available to play in a game.

The Offense

Five big, quick players called linemen form the offensive team's front line. This offensive line includes the center, two guards, and two tackles. The center snaps the ball to the quarterback between his legs and calls out positions to his fellow linemen. The whole line's job is then to block the defense. These players open running lanes, or holes, for teammates carrying the ball. They also protect the quarterback as he or she passes the ball.

The quarterback stands behind the center, ready for the ball.

A quarterback prepares to pass to a teammate.

The quarterback is the leader of the offense. The quarterback calls plays, throws passes, runs with the ball, and hands off the ball to the two running backs. These running backs, a fullback and a halfback, run with the ball. They may also throw passes. Three ends—one tight end and two wide receivers—run down the field to catch the football. The tight end lines up next to the offensive linemen and helps block opponents.

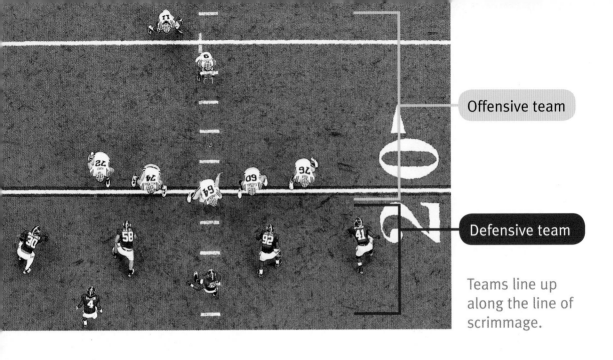

Offensive team

Defensive team

Teams line up along the line of scrimmage.

The Defense

Four powerful, agile players—two tackles and two ends—make up the defensive line. A defensive tackle's job is to grab and bring down ball carriers. Defensive ends are smaller and faster than tackles. Their job is to crash through the offensive line to reach the ball carrier or the quarterback. Three linebackers are positioned behind the defensive linemen. They stop running plays and cover receivers on passing plays.

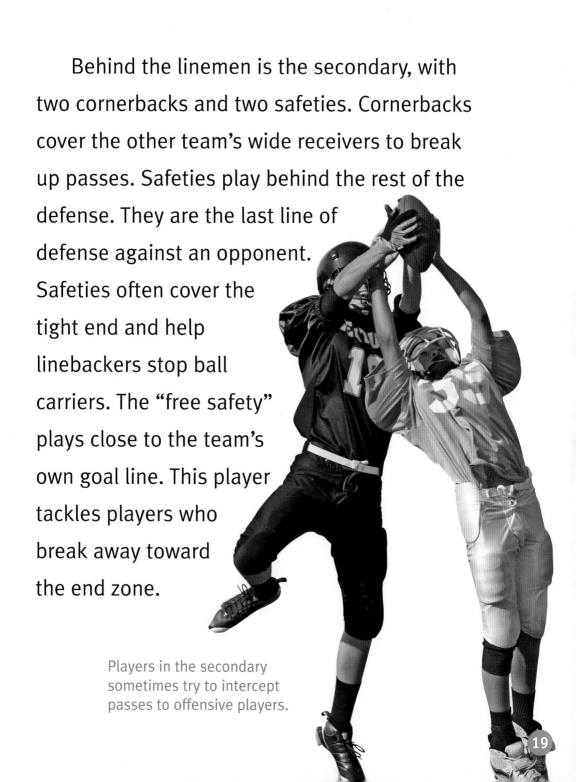

Behind the linemen is the secondary, with two cornerbacks and two safeties. Cornerbacks cover the other team's wide receivers to break up passes. Safeties play behind the rest of the defense. They are the last line of defense against an opponent. Safeties often cover the tight end and help linebackers stop ball carriers. The "free safety" plays close to the team's own goal line. This player tackles players who break away toward the end zone.

Players in the secondary sometimes try to intercept passes to offensive players.

19

Special Teams

Special teams take the field during kicking plays such as kickoffs and punts. These units of players include kickers who boot kickoffs, extra points, and field goal attempts. Punters kick, or punt, the ball to the opponent. There are also kick returners, who catch kicked balls and run them toward the opponent's goal line. A holder is responsible for holding the ball upright for the kicker to kick extra points and field goals.

Rules protect a holder and kicker from being tackled by the other team.

Evolution of the Football

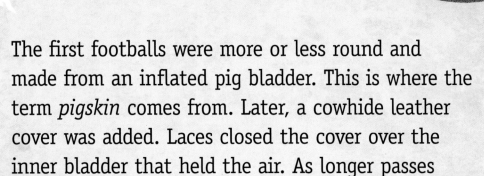

The first footballs were more or less round and made from an inflated pig bladder. This is where the term *pigskin* comes from. Later, a cowhide leather cover was added. Laces closed the cover over the inner bladder that held the air. As longer passes grew more common in the early 1900s, the ball became slimmer and its ends more pointed. This improved a pass's accuracy. The laces on modern footballs do not hold the ball together. Instead, they allow players to grip the ball and throw it more accurately.

Women of the Gridiron

Women's tackle football is not new—it's been around for more than four decades! The three current **leagues** include teams from the United States and Canada.

The rules are much the same as in men's football. Full-contact tackles are standard. Most teams also play with 11 players on the field. In one **division**, teams of eight play one another.

While NFL games are played in huge stadiums across the country, the women's league usually plays on high school fields or at smaller stadiums and sports complexes. The players don't receive the men's paychecks, either. Women players pay to play, covering equipment, travel, and other costs themselves.

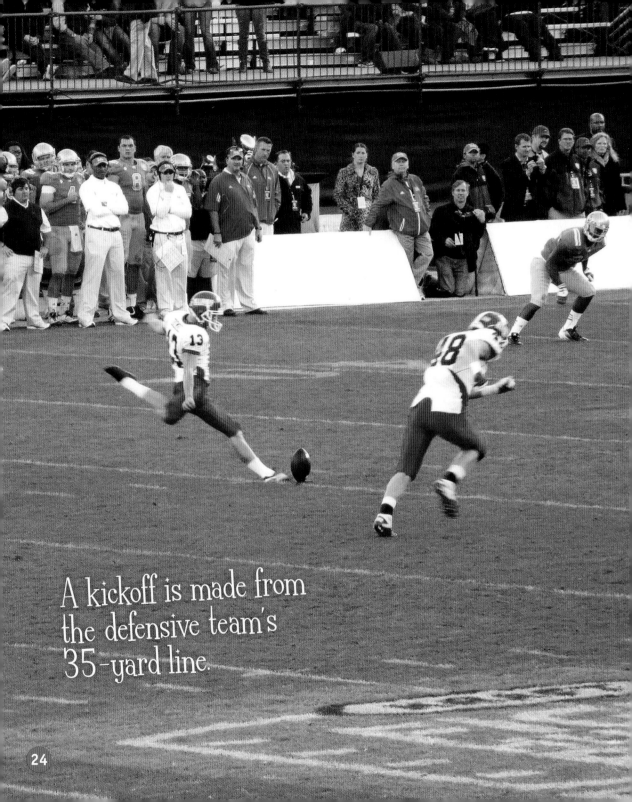

A kickoff is made from the defensive team's 35-yard line.

CHAPTER 4

Rules and Regulations

A football game begins with a kickoff. The kicker on the defensive team kicks the ball to the kickoff returner of the offensive team. The returner runs with the ball as far up the field as possible before being tackled or stepping out of bounds. At that point, the play is over. The location of the tackle or out-of-bounds step becomes the line of scrimmage. This is the starting point for the offensive team's first play.

On the March

The offensive team can run or pass the ball through the opposition's territory, toward the goal line. The team's goal is to enter the opponent's end zone for a touchdown. The offense has four plays, called downs, to move the ball at least 10 yards (9 m) from the line of scrimmage. If it succeeds, it is awarded a new set of four downs. If it fails, it may use its fourth down to punt the ball or try for a field goal.

Timeline of Football History

1869

First college football game in the United States is played.

1922

The National Football League (NFL) forms with 18 teams.

1959

The American Football League (AFL) forms; the first AFL game is played the following year.

Scoring

Field goal kicks are worth three points. A two-point safety goes to the defensive team when a ball carrier is tackled in his or her own end zone. A touchdown earns the most points, at six. After a touchdown, the scoring team may try for extra points in one of two ways. A field goal earns one point. Running or passing the ball into the end zone again from the 2-yard line earns the team two points.

1967
First AFL-NFL championship game is played; the game is later renamed the Super Bowl.

1970
The NFL and the AFL merge to form a 26-team league called the NFL.

Present
NFL membership includes 32 teams.

Basic Rules

Rules protect the players' safety and ensure the game is fair. For example, players cannot kick, punch, or trip an opponent or grab an opponent's face mask. Jumping on top of a ball carrier who has been tackled is not allowed either.

If a rule is broken, officials signal, or call, a penalty. They throw a yellow flag onto the ground where the **infraction** occurred. The team that broke the rule loses yards or a down.

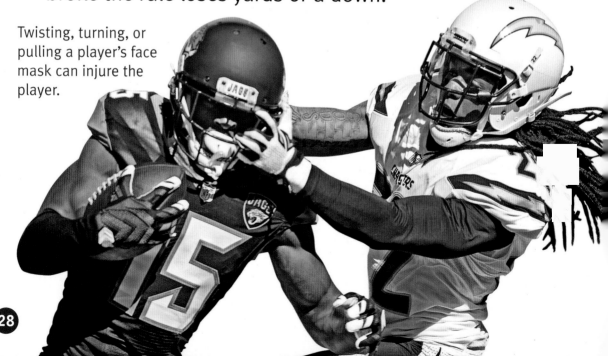

Twisting, turning, or pulling a player's face mask can injure the player.

Hand Signals

Football officials use hand signals to let the fans know what happens on the field. To signal a touchdown, for example, the official extends both arms straight up (left). The official grabs one wrist with the other hand and pulls down the arm to signal a **holding** penalty (right). To signal pass **interference**, the official extends both arms straight forward (below).

Play Like the Pros

There are roughly 1.1 million high school football players in the United States. About 250,000 football players ages 5 to 15 years are in youth leagues. Because it's a contact sport, however, playing football involves some risk. Today, the NFL and other football organizations are working to make the sport safer than ever. If you have permission to play, develop your skills to the fullest. Above all, play safely and have fun!

 Football players weren't required to wear a helmet until 1943.

Passing

Making strong, accurate passes begins with the proper grip of the football. Grip the ball with three fingers on the laces. Your thumb should be underneath, toward the tip of the ball. The index finger is behind the laces. You'll want to control the ball with your fingertips, so don't let the ball rest in the palm of your hand. Fingertip control will help you throw a good spiral that travels quickly.

If your hand is small, you can hold the ball closer to its point for a better grip.

Make sure you follow through after you release the ball.

To begin your throw, raise the ball to ear level and behind your head. Move the leg opposite your throwing arm to the direction you want to pass. Point your free hand toward the receiver and turn your hips toward him. Move your throwing arm forward with your wrist stiff. Keep the foot opposite your throwing arm on the ground. Release the ball just past your head. Follow through with your throwing arm and body.

Rushing

Running with the ball toward the opponent's end zone is called rushing. It often starts with a handoff from the quarterback. Hold both forearms horizontal and close to your chest. One forearm should be higher, palm facing down. The lower palm should face up. The quarterback forces the ball into this "pocket." Hold the ball tightly with both hands against your body. Look for any running lanes through the defense and move toward one quickly.

Close your arms around the ball as you receive the handoff.

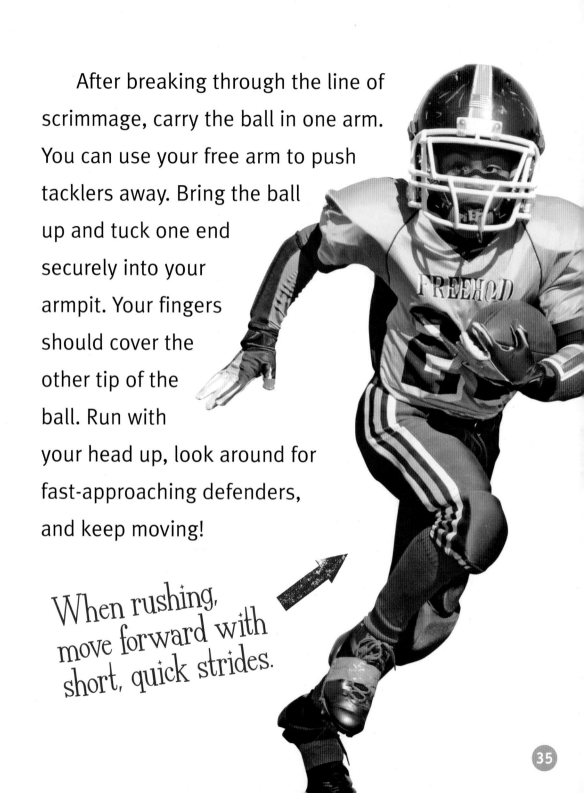

After breaking through the line of scrimmage, carry the ball in one arm. You can use your free arm to push tacklers away. Bring the ball up and tuck one end securely into your armpit. Your fingers should cover the other tip of the ball. Run with your head up, look around for fast-approaching defenders, and keep moving!

When rushing, move forward with short, quick strides.

If a pass is high, you may have to jump for it.

Receiving

Great receivers catch the ball with their hands, not their body. To catch a high pass, form a triangle shape with the tips of your thumbs and index fingers. Spread your fingers, and catch the ball in this "web" you've created. If a pass is low, you'll have to bend to catch it. Create a "scoop" with your pinkies together and palms up. After catching the ball, bring it into your body. Hold it tightly with your fingers and thumbs.

Tackling

Solid defense requires great tackling. The ball carrier may come directly at you, or you might chase the player from the side or from behind. No matter what, keep your head up. Your eyes should be on that person at all times. Grab the runner by the waist or thighs and thrust your shoulder into the person's body. Tightly wrap your arms around the ball carrier and use the power in your legs to drive the player toward the ground.

Sometimes, a person dives at a ball carrier to make a tackle.

Legendary running back Jim Brown played for the Cleveland Browns in the 1950s and 1960s.

CHAPTER 6

Gridiron Greats

Being a professional football player requires strength, speed, dedication, intelligence, and hard work. Players work year-round to keep in shape and sharpen their skills. Thousands of athletes have played in the National Football League since it was formed almost 100 years ago. Of that number, relatively few make it to the top of their profession. Only the best can be considered a "gridiron great."

The NFL has nearly 1,700 active players each year.

Legendary Offensive Players

Many people consider Jim Brown the greatest running back in the history of the NFL. In his nine-year career, he led the league in number of yards rushed eight times. Brown also won Rookie of the Year and Most Valuable Player (MVP) awards. Running back Walter Payton could outrun, smash into, and plow over defenders. An MVP award winner, Payton ranks second in all-time career rushing with 16,726 yards (15.3 km).

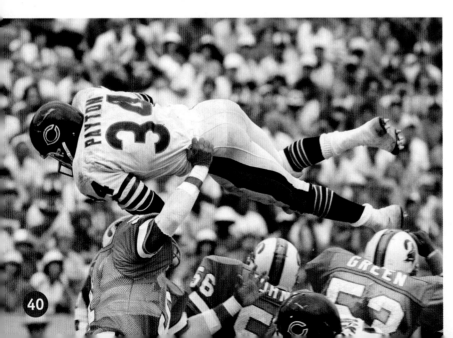

Walter Payton, playing for the Chicago Bears, leaps over players on a rush to the end zone. He played for the Bears in the 1970s and 1980s.

Anthony Muñoz (center) played for the Cincinnati Bengals for 12 years, starting in 1980.

Peyton Manning attempts to pass the ball.

Joe Montana, Tom Brady, and Peyton Manning are among the greatest quarterbacks. Montana and Brady have each guided their teams to four Super Bowl championships. Manning holds the records for most career touchdowns thrown and most career passing yards. Wide receiver Jerry Rice holds the career receptions record with 1,549 catches. He is also a three-time Super Bowl champ. Many experts consider offensive tackle Anthony Muñoz the greatest offensive lineman in NFL history.

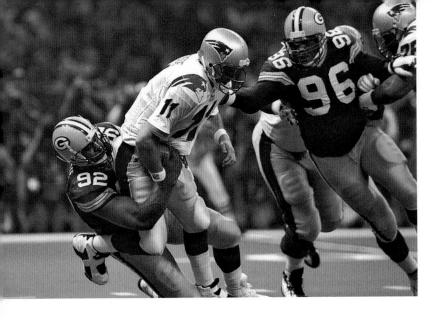

Reggie White (number 92) pulls down a Patriots ball carrier. White played for the Green Bay Packers in the 1990s. He spent 8 years with the Philadelphia Eagles before that.

Legendary Defensive Players

Linebacker Lawrence Taylor combined strength and speed. One of the NFL's greatest pass rushers, Taylor was a two-time Super Bowl champion. Defensive end Reggie White used his size—6 feet 5 inches (1.9 m), 300 pounds (136 kg)—and quickness. Nicknamed the Minister of Defense, White is second in number of sacks in a career. A sack occurs when a defensive player tackles the quarterback behind the line of scrimmage as the quarterback tries to pass the ball.

Defensive end J. J. Watt was the first NFL player with two seasons of 20 or more sacks. With his all-around athletic ability, Watt has also played offense as a tight end. Deion Sanders ranks among the NFL's greatest cornerbacks. The two-time Super Bowl champ also returned punts and kicks. Ronnie Lott is considered one of the best cornerbacks. He also played safety. During his 14-year career, Lott won four Super Bowl championships. All of these players are great examples of being your best at football. ★

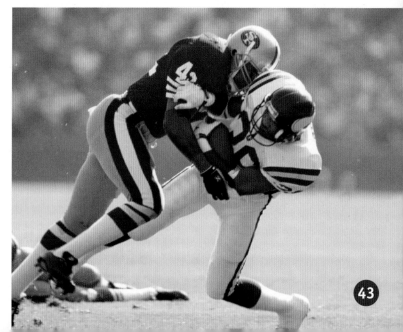

Ronnie Lott smashes into a ball carrier. Lott spent most of his career in the 1980s and 1990s with the San Francisco 49ers.

True Statistics

Most seasons played in the NFL by a single player: 26, George Blanda

Most touchdowns scored by a player in a single season: 31, by LaDainian Tomlinson in 2006

Most yards gained by a player in a single season: 2,105, by Eric Dickerson in 1984

Most points scored by an NFL team during a Super Bowl: 55, by the San Francisco 49ers during Super Bowl XXIV in 1990

Fewest points scored by an NFL team during a Super Bowl: 3, by the Miami Dolphins during Super Bowl VI in 1972

Length of the longest play in NFL history: 109 yards (100m), by Antonio Cromartie in 2007 in a return from a missed field goal

Average attendance for an NFL game: 67,000

Weight of the heaviest player in NFL history: 410 lbs. (186 kg), Aaron Gibson

Did you find the truth?

(T) Players are required to wear protective gear when playing football.

(F) Only men play professional football.

Resources

Books

Der, Bob, ed. *Sports Illustrated Kids Big Book of Who: Football*. New York: Time Home Entertainment, 2013.

Jacobs, Greg. *The Everything Kids' Football Book: The All-Time Greats, Legendary Teams, and Today's Favorite Players—With Tips on Playing Like a Pro*. Avon, MA: Adams Media, 2014.

Kelley, K. C. *Quarterback Superstars 2015*. New York: Scholastic, 2015.

Visit this Scholastic Web site for more information on being your best at football:
★ www.factsfornow.scholastic.com
Enter the keywords **Being Your Best at Football**

Important Words

cleats (KLEETS) metal or wooden spikes fastened to the bottom of a shoe or boot to prevent slipping

contact sport (KAHN-takt SPORT) an activity in which physical contact is a normal part of game play

division (dih-VIZH-uhn) group of teams within a larger league that play one another

endurance (en-DOOR-uhns) the ability to do something difficult for a long time

gridiron (GRID-eye-urn) a playing field marked by evenly spaced parallel lines for football

holding (HOLD-ing) an illegal move in which a player holds, pulls, or grabs another player who does not hold the ball

infraction (in-FRAK-shun) a breaking of a rule

interference (in-tur-FEER-uhns) the illegal blocking of an opponent

leagues (LEEGZ) groups of sports teams, usually professional

opponent (uh-POH-nuhnt) the person or team you play or compete against

professional (pruh-FESH-uhn-ul) making money for doing something others do for fun

synthetic (sin-THET-ik) manufactured or human made, rather than found in nature

Index

Page numbers in **bold** indicate illustrations.

About the Author

Nel Yomtov is an award-winning author with a passion for writing nonfiction books for young readers. He has written books and graphic novels about history, geography, science, and other subjects.

Nel has worked at Marvel Comics, where he edited, wrote, and colored hundreds of titles. He has also served as editorial director of a children's book publisher and as publisher of Hammond World Atlas books.

Yomtov lives in the New York City area with his wife, Nancy, a teacher. Their son, Jess, is a sports journalist.

OCT 2 8 2018